What Has Beak?

by Will Lawrence

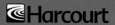Harcourt

Orlando   Boston   Dallas   Chicago   San Diego

Visit *The Learning Site!*

www.harcourtschool.com

What has a beak?

A bird has a beak.

What has feathers?

A bird has feathers.

What has wings?

A bird has wings.

A bird can fly.